To: Ginger
Be You!

Be Understanding

An Escaping the friend Zone Novella

THIA FINN

Be Understanding
An Escaping the Friend Zone Novella

Thia Finn

ALL RIGHTS RESERVED. This book contains material protected under the International and Federal Copyright Laws and Treaties. **Any unauthorized reprint or use of this material is prohibited.** No part of this book may be reproduced or transmitted in any form or by any means, electronic or mechanical, including photocopying, recording, or by any information storage and retrieval system without express written permission from the author/publisher.

FILE SHARING: Please note that this book is protected under the Digital Millennium Copyright Act (DMCA). It has been made available for your personal use and enjoyment. **No permission has been granted to upload this book onto ANY file-sharing websites.** Doing so is a violation of federal laws and measures have been taken within this file to track the originator of such shared files, should it be found on piracy sites. Thank you for respecting the hard work of the author to produce this content.

WARNING: This is a work of fiction. Names, characters, businesses, places, events and incidents are either the products of the author's imagination or used in a fictitious manner. Any resemblance to actual persons, living or dead, or actual events is purely coincidental.

ISBN13: 978-796374568

Edited by Swish Design & Editing
Proofreading by Swish Design & Editing
Book designed and formatted by Swish Design & Editing
Cover Design by More Than Words Graphic Design
Cover Image Copyright 2019

Copyright © 2019 Thia Finn
All rights reserved.

This book is dedicated to all the authors who have helped me move forward in this crazy writing career. They offer me help in many forms without expecting anything in return. I would still be working on my first book without them. Thank you!

Be Understanding

An Escaping the Friend Zone Novella

Be Understanding

"What are you doing back here by yourself, Skyla?"

I hung my head between my knees hoping Rett would get the message. The last thing I needed right now was having to explain myself to him. With his knee brushing against mine as he squatted beside me, I felt Rett before I saw him. The clean woodsy scent surrounded me giving away who stood there. This guy always smelled the best. The female fans even wrote long Facebook posts about how luscious his scent was when they briefly encountered him from the front of the stage. I had watched him lean down and shake a hand or wipe his brow with some scrap of material the dreaming female had handed him. Sometimes he even kissed the object or pretended to. The longing looks in their eyes told him they were his for the taking with nothing more than a nod of the head. From the wings of the stage, anyone could see his interactions with his fans.

Being a roadie on this tour, I had more than enough opportunity to log his signature fragrance in my brain. He spent time around us at each show. His idea of loading in and out was more hands-on than most of the other band members.

Rett never directed us or stepped on the toes of our boss, Dex, but he always stood around to lend a hand if needed. His guitar held more importance to him than any woman attached to his side, so watching it take its honored position on stage became necessary to him with each show.

"I'm fine, Rett. I know you have a lot to do. The others talked about the after-party at some club. You should be there by now." My voice sounded monotone even to me. I spoke without raising my head because he needed to get the idea I wanted to be alone.

"Nah, I'm thinking of skipping it tonight. I'm exhausted. This venue might as well have been a fucking spot in the desert. The heat takes the life out of me." He slid down the wall sitting beside me, our hips and legs rubbing together. "So tell me, why are you out here, Skyla?"

It felt weird talking to him with my head down, so I slowly raised it but never looked at him. The red welt on the other side of my face would remain hidden. "It's just that…" I sucked in a heavy breath trying to keep the tears at bay, "… I had a hard time tonight."

His eyes burned a hole in the side of my face. "Who or what gave you shit tonight?"

Becks

"It's fine, Rett. I don't really want to talk about it." The ragged sound my voice made gave more away than I wanted it to.

"Skyla, I don't have many friends these days with all the traveling we do, but you've been one of them since the band hired the company you work for. You know you can tell me anything."

"Oh, yeah? Well, I'm glad you feel that way because a real friend wouldn't hound me for answers I don't want to talk about." Turning his words back on him could possibly convince him I didn't want to talk.

"Okay, okay, I get it. We don't have to talk about why you're out here then. We can talk about something else."

"How about you go to your party, and I'll go do my job instead?"

"Now, what's the fun in that?"

Rett had always been sweet to me even when the other band members acted like dicks most of the time. His friendly attitude put me at ease from day one. While the others tried to hit on me when it was convenient for them, his way of approaching or talking to me didn't sound like a line of bullshit the others all had.

Being a female roadie didn't make me easy. In my eyes, it made me the opposite. The idea of hooking up with the guys in the band or the others working for the company held no appeal.

My job suited me fine. I studied music for years and wanted to be in a band but that kind of job never materialized, so I did the next best thing by being a roadie. At least, the opportunity to be around music existed with the job.

"I'm sure the females you promised you'd see later have a much better answer for you." I glanced in his direction to see his reaction, careful to keep the stinging side of my face hidden.

"Why don't we sneak off and do something fun? It'll take your mind off whatever's bothering you, and I won't be the center of attraction for a change. Let the other guys have the spotlight at the party tonight."

"Are you forgetting I have a job to do?" I never shirked my responsibilities because I knew the company would replace me in a heartbeat. If Dex reported me for skipping out on work, I would be shipped home.

"Oh, little lady, are you forgetting I'm the boss's boss, and can change his plans for you any minute I choose?" His smile took up his entire face. He popped those dimples when he really wanted to turn on the charm. The slight dips in his tanned cheeks told me he wanted me to believe him.

"Right, but then I'll be paying for it later."

"What does that mean?" Concern oozed with each word as the crease between his eyebrows appeared.

"It means he will be watching my every move after we return to make sure I toe the line at the next stop. I don't like him watching me that closely. Gives me the creeps."

He let out a deep breath. "Yeah, I can see that."

Becks

"Well, if you won't come with me to have some fun now then let's go get your job finished, and then we'll go. I'm not feeling an after-party at all tonight." He stood and offered me his hand.

As I hesitated, I looked up at him forgetting about my cheek.

Seeing his face change I knew instantly I'd made a mistake.

"What the fuck, Skyla?" He grabbed my shoulders and lifted me to stand in front of him. "Did Dex do this to you?"

My hand covered the mark. "No, no he didn't."

"Then who did? I'll make sure they never work for this company again."

"It's okay, Rett. Let it go."

"No, I will not let it go. No man is going to abuse any woman on my tour, and you shouldn't be okay with it either."

With my feelings hovering near the surface I couldn't stop the tears that spilled over and flowed over my cheeks. They only made matters worse in his eyes. *Why did I let things like this bother me?*

"I'll take care of it in my own way, Rett. Besides, who said it was a man who did it?"

"You let a woman hit you? I don't believe it." His wide eye stare and the stern look on his face scared me.

Keeping my cheek covered, I nodded my head. "It's not like I let her do it. It just happened when I wasn't expecting it. The slap left me shocked so I couldn't respond before she took off."

"Who. Did. This?" His staggered words heightened my fear even more.

"I'd rather not say, Rett. Let me take care of it, please?" My entire face felt red now. God, what a dumbass I must look like to him.

He glanced down the empty hallway before he turned back to me. "Whoever did this is wrong, Skyla. You know that, right?"

Again, I nodded. What he said made complete sense to me now, but when it happened she caught me completely off guard. She kept her temper in check out in public most of the time and never had she done something so rash when one of the band was around. The idea of being caught might scare her, but I doubted it.

I still had no idea why she did it this time. Having someone else fight my battles wasn't the way I ever handled things.

Rett wrapped his big arm around my neck and turned. "Come on, then. You need a night out for fun, and I saw just the place for that to happen on the drive in this morning."

"I told you I need to get back to work."

We took a few steps toward the stage area. "You want to have to tell an entire crew about your face?" My head jerked in his direction. "That's what I thought. If you go back in there now everyone's going to start asking questions." He studied my cheek up close. "It's still blood red, Skyla. So, it's go with me out the door to fun, or answer questions you're not prepared for. What's it going to be?"

I stared at him trying to make up my mind. I didn't want to answer questions, so guessed I had nothing to decide. "I'll go with you, but I still need to tell Dex I'm leaving."

Rett pulled his phone from his pocket. "I'll text him telling him I'm taking you with me, that way there'll be no questions for him to ask tomorrow."

"Thanks, I think."

Chapter 2

The carnival's lights captured my attention from miles away. As the loud Harley came to a stop at the side of the road, I turned to see him looking back at me.

"You've gotta get off here. That sand is too unstable to ride this big hog through. Last thing we need to do is lay it over." Rett put a hand up for me to grab and slide off. The vibrations of the engine continued through me as I stood and watched him get off and push it forward to a safe parking spot.

The bright colors of the lights mesmerized me. I couldn't remember the last time I went to a carnival like this one. The sound of the carnies yelling out from their booths grew louder as we got closer.

"So, what do you think? Can I pick fun or what?" Rett's smile said it all. The little kid in him surfaced with each step. "Let's get a string of tickets and play them all."

Becks

"Oh, I don't know. I'm not good at these things. The booth always used to take my money when I was a kid."

"Not me. I bet I can beat them all. We'll be giving away stuffed animals to all the little kids running around." He pointed to the squealing kids jumping up and down in the midway before us.

"Bragging much?" I laughingly asked.

"Not bragging, I'm good at this. There's a trick to winning them."

Rett made good on the suggestion and came back to me with a small roll of tickets.

"Rett, you meant what you said about playing every game. It'll take forever to use that many tickets."

"Hell, yeah, I did. We came to have fun, so let's get to it, girl."

Some women would take offense at being called girl by a grown man but not me, and certainly not coming from Rett. He'd been nothing but friendly and kind to me since we'd met. The day before my first tour with Sharp Edges we all met at the warehouse. The equipment that traveled with the band took up a lot of space. The band hired the company I worked for to travel with them. It was my first time being part of a real tour like Sharp Edges—it was first class everything.

All of the members of the band showed to meet us and appeared to be nice, but their true personalities didn't pop out until we were on the road. Each one had a way they wanted things done, and it was up to us to work around their idiosyncrasies.

I got along with them all, after they figured out sleeping with any of them was out of the question. A couple tried harder than others, but it was all good now.

Rett was not one of the two, and that made it easier to be friends with him sooner than the others. He spoke to me like we were equals, instead of down to me like some of the band members and the roadies did.

"Come on, Skyla. Let's go ride the rides first. I don't want to have to buy a seat for a huge teddy bear, too." He grabbed my hand and pulled me to the rides at the end of the midway.

We stood in line and waited for the tilt-a-whirl. I watched the others in line around us to see if any of them picked up on who Rett was. Thankfully, he had on a ball-cap and some fake glasses to help hide his appearance. No one seemed to take any notice which made us both happy.

The last thing either of us wanted to do was outrun a crowd of fans. Those people could go from friendly to crazy in a New York minute.

I leaned in and whispered, "Glad you thought to bring the glasses."

He nodded without looking up at me keeping his back turned away from the line, and I kept us moving forward.

When our turn came, he pushed me forward to the open door. I might have needed a little more nudging than some. Just thinking about whirling and twirling inside a metal cage made me a little sick but I was determined to do it. Rett was excited to ride, and I wouldn't spoil his fun for anything.

"You ready?" he asked, and I closed my eyes and took a deep breath. "I hope you don't plan to keep your eyes closed the whole time. You'll be barfing all over both of us." He laughed out loud.

"No. If you must know I was praying," I said with a perfectly straight face and gave him my best attempt at a glare.

He immediately dropped the smile. "Oh, I'm sorry. I didn't realize."

I busted out laughing. "Oh. My. God. You're too easy, Rett."

"Well, I didn't know if you must know, maybe you were religious or something. I mean, no one's ever said anything about it, but I can get behind it if you are."

I reached over and patted his cheek. "No worries. I'm not all that religious, but if it helps to keep us from dying inside this cage I'll pray for the both of us."

He stared hard at me. "Are you really joking right now before this thing takes off?" His serious face caught me off guard. Then he started laughing again. "See, two can play your game."

We both laughed as the ride jerked to a start. The cage began to move forward before rocking and then rolling over and over. I screamed and Rett screamed, and then we laughed at each other before our screams started in earnest. When it finally came to sudden stop, I felt like my body had been battered and bruised from all the flinging from side to side inside the metal.

Rett reached up and rubbed the side of his head. "I think you put a bruise on me."

"No, that's what you did to me." I rubbed my nose. "Maybe you broke my nose." We looked at each other and laughed again.

The rest of the rides only added to our aches and pains until we came to the Ferris wheel. We'd purposely saved it for last because it was the tamest ride on the lot. As we approached it, I glanced up at Rett. His face turned upward looking at how high the wheel sat as it waited to come down the backside to the ground.

"I think this is the tallest ride here," he commented as I followed his eyes up to the top car.

"Yeah, I'm not afraid of heights. You?"

"I'm not too wild about them, but it'll be great to see the city from up there." We both kept our thoughts to ourselves until we were locking the bar down over our laps. "You ready for this, little girl?"

"I'm not a little girl, Rett." I couldn't resist telling him that. I wanted to say more but changed my mind. Better for him to think of me that way than anything else. He looked over at me but didn't say more.

As we were the last of the new riders, we took off for several rotations before it came to a stop to let off riders.

Becks

"This is the part I hate the most," he quietly said. Our car was about half way up, and we had to go up and over stopping at each car.

"Let's talk about something to take our minds off it then."

He turned to me. "Okay, how about we start with you telling me about yourself. We travel together all the time, and I don't know anything about you.

"What do you want to know?"

"Why you took the job as a roadie? It's hard work and a thankless task."

"I've been playing music all my life. I went to school thinking I'd be a music major and play in some awesome band sooner or later."

"Did you finish? What happened to keep you from doing that?"

"No, I had to drop out because of money. My parents cut me off when they realized I planned to join a band when I graduated."

"They didn't want you using the degree for something you loved?"

"No, they wanted me to find a husband. You know, major is M.R.S. instead of a BS in Music."

Rett laughed at my attempt at a dumb joke. The sad part was it wasn't a joke. "So, they expected you to come back with a husband instead of a degree? I guess I've never heard of that degree plan before. I never went to college."

"The small local university I attended had a great music department, but an even greater opportunity to find a husband as far as they were concerned."

"Probably a good thing I didn't go then. Some momma might have set her sights set on me to achieve that dream with. I'm not looking to get married anytime soon."

I punched him with my elbow in an easy way. "You still living with that love 'em and leave 'em mentality that rockers are famous for?"

"Damn straight I am. Last thing I want right now is someone else to worry about. When I find 'the one' that'll be it for me, but have you seen me with that many women since you've been on tour with us?" I shrugged. "I'm not one to date. Never have been. I didn't even go out in high school. My mom made me go to the prom or I wouldn't have gone."

He looked at me. "We were supposed to be talking about you, not me. How'd you do that?"

Our car rocked at the very top and my lips eased into a smile. "Caught on to that did ya?" We both laughed as I peered over the side and down.

"Don't do that, Skyla. It scares the hell out of me just watching you."

"It's fine, I promise." My comment drifted over my shoulder.

"Not to me." He pulled on my arm to return me flat onto the bench and wrapped his arm around my shoulders holding me in place. He kept it there making me wonder if it was intentional.

Becks

Gazing at him, I realized the terrified look on his face was real, and that I needed to change the subject. "Look at the skyline instead. It's beautiful from here." We both stared out at the downtown area. The buildings' lights brightened the sky in a variety of colors. It made a gorgeous sight to capture his attention.

"What about you? Did you go to prom? I bet you were the prom queen or something." His voice brought me back to the moment.

The look I gave him said it all. "Uh... no," I added.

"But you went, right?"

"Oh, yeah. My parents insisted it was a rite of passage and not attending was out of the question."

"Sounds like it wasn't the fun event they pitched to convince you to go."

"Anything but..." I refused to give him anything extra about the horrific night.

"Did you go with the prom king or something and he ditched you? You make it sound like it was the worst night of your life."

"It was."

God, how did I get myself into conversations better left in the past?

"Come on, Skyla. Friends share these horror stories so you can laugh at them after all these years."

With the pleading look on his face, I knew he wouldn't laugh at me... too much.

"A guy asked me out who I'd been doing some flirting with for a while. We had a nice date, nothing too exciting though. The next day he asked me to go to prom with him, and I hadn't been asked so it thrilled me to know I would go with a date and not friends. We didn't hang out with the same crowd at school, but I thought we could still have a good time. Over the next month or so, we dated and spent time with his friends on the football team and their girlfriends. None of the girls were particularly nice to me but they weren't total bitches either, so I decided they were only trying to get to know me.

We spent time alone, you know, doing the heavy making out thing along the way but we never had sex, and he didn't push it either. The night of the prom we went with a group in a limo. We took pictures at one of the girls' gorgeous homes in a high dollar neighborhood. When we got in the limo, it was stocked with all kinds of alcohol. I'd never really drunk before, so we started with a glass of champagne, I had a glass to be social. You know, I didn't want to look like a total geek in front of the 'cool kids.'

"Sounds like it started out like a fun night. What's one glass of champagne?" I glanced around and saw we were making our way down the backside of the wheel, so telling this stupid story helped keep Rett's mind occupied. His arm around me felt good, too.

"Yeah, it would have been if everyone had stopped there. By the time we made it to the ballroom, some of them had done shots, and a few had passed around a couple of joints.

Becks

I watched them hold the smoke inside and then blow it out. Being the nerdy one of the group, I'd never even seen marijuana before. I had no clue what to do with it. When they passed it to me, my first instinct was to say no, but it felt like they all watched to see what I would do. Naturally, I let the peer pressure get the best of me and tried sucking in a lungful. Guess you know how that ended?"

Rett laughed a little. "Coughing fit, huh?"

"Hell, yeah. That shit burned every inch of the way down."

"That's not a good way to start, Skyla. The asshat you were with should have told you not to do that."

"Yeah, well... turned out, he didn't tell me a lot of things he should have." I stopped thinking of the disaster the night continued to be as the soft rocking of the car continued.

"Hey, go on... you're not at the good part yet."

My head whipped around. "How do you know that's not the good part?"

"Because I can see those wheels in your head spinning every time I look at you."

I smiled. "Right. So anyway, by the time we arrived most of the people in the limo were loaded, stoned, something... I shrugged. "I felt like throwing up from breathing in the second-hand smoke."

"Boxing can do that to you, although some people think it's impossible. But that's another story. Keep going."

The look on my face must have said 'weirdo' because he started laughing again. I needed to get out into the world more, but if traveling with a bunch of musicians didn't do it for me then what would?

"Sooo…" I purposely dragged the word out, "… the actual time at the dance proved to be the best time of the night. We danced together, apart, and with any and everyone around us. The guys, and probably the girls from the limo, continued to drink from flasks they had snuck in. Our chaperones must have been paid to look the other way at the door because they checked our purses but nothing on the guys."

"Damn, I wish the teachers at ours would've considered taking money for that. They'd make enough to live on for the year."

"Yeah, well, it was all good until they crowned the king and queen, who happened to be part of the crowd I had arrived with. While we stood there watching, I noticed the guys all huddled beside me comparing something from their pockets. Turned out to be the keycards to the rooms someone had rented. One was the penthouse which had three bedrooms. No one asked if I wanted to go to an after-party. The girls invited me to spend the night at one of their houses. How was I supposed to know that was code for actually staying in a hotel room with my date?"

"Oh, now, come on, Skyla. Surely you had to know something was going down when you spotted the keycards?"

"I asked my date about it and he said it was for the after-party, and we'd only go for a little bit and then we'd Uber to Jillian's house." I stopped and looked at Rett. The story only went downhill from here and I hated repeating it. "Anyway, we rode the elevator to the top floor in silence. My mind created every possible scenario on the way, but nothing I invented came close to the actual events.

"I heard the loud laughing when the elevator doors opened right into the party. People stood around drinking and smoking more joints. Everyone had lost their formal clothes for something less restrictive, like panties and bras, boxers, and a few girls in thongs only. Guess they didn't wear bras that night under their dresses. When my date started undoing his bowtie, I squeaked. Literally squeaked. It caused everyone in the room to turn and look at us. He unbuttoned his shirt and then glanced over at me like he expected me to do the same."

"Bet that was shocking to your delicate sensitivities."

"Don't make fun of me, Rett. I was traumatized from that moment on."

"Oh, yeah? Did he do a Magic Mike scene for you or something?"

"Something like that. He slid his hand behind me and started pulling at the zipper on my dress. It stopped from the material getting hung up about halfway down. He called to one of the girls to come help him. I stood there letting it happen. A whole group got behind me and started on my zipper. Thank God they didn't break it in their drunken molesting of the delicate lace. With all of their laughing and wild efforts, the whole room stared at me for my unveiling.

"My mother insisted I wear a strapless bra. I silently thanked her when the dress fell to the floor, and everyone in the room cheered. My skin turned as red as the lace of my matching bra and panties she made me buy." I turned and gave Rett a hard stare. "Do you think my mom knew ahead of time what was going to happen? I never thought about that fact before now. Oh. My. God. My mother expected me to have sex on the night of my prom. Can you believe that?"

"Well, no, but since I don't know your mom it's hard for me to answer that."

"I had a curfew until the day I left home. How could she look the other way for that one night?"

"Maybe she wanted you to have a real experience for a change from the rest of your high school days. How old were you?"

"Eighteen. My birthday's in December. We were both eighteen, his right after he asked me to it. He went out with his friends that night and I was happy about it. I knew they would get into some things I didn't want to be involved in."

"So, you were both consenting adults, Skyla. Did he force you to have sex? Was it a rape? Did he get you drunk and force himself on you? If that's where this story is going, I'm calling the airlines and making your hometown or wherever he is now my next stop. I'll beat the shit out of him for doing that."

I couldn't lie to him. "Slow down, alpha dog. I never said the word 'rape.'"

Becks

"Thank God. I hate to have to fly off to do a beatdown on a stranger, but for you I'd have done it."

"I'm flattered, Rett, truly. But nothing of the sort happened. Just the opposite, really."

His eyebrows got those creased lines between them again. I'd seen it happen a few times during their sound checks but never realized it was a tell for him.

"So finish, please. I'm sorry for interrupting and acting all badass."

"Well, after my unveiling of sorts, I realized my average sized breasts didn't impress anyone nearly as much as the girls who had already gotten the fake boobs in our senior year. They all went back to carrying on and partying. My date disappeared in his heart boxers to get a beer. He checked on me from time to time but when I saw him going into one of the bedrooms with fake boobs and his best friend, I decided it was time for me to go home. I took my dress to the entryway and slid back into it and I Ubered home alone.

"When my parents asked why I didn't spend the night at the friend's house, I lied and told her they wanted to sneak out and drink so I came home. Now that I think about it, I believe my mother was disappointed in me. We never talked about it, but the school on Monday morning couldn't let it go. Apparently, my date came looking for me to have next in the bedroom and found my dress gone. Then he kindly announced to the entire party that the little goodie-two-shoes he planned to bone the virginity out of had skipped out on him and he was pissed about it. Told the entire baseball team at practice on Monday that I gave him a blow job and he hated it, so I left."

"Damn, Skyla, you left out the blowing him part."

"That's because it didn't happen. He convinced the team that my skills lacked anyway. Needless to say, my Saturday nights until graduation consisted of hanging out with girlfriends and my parents. The only thing different was the guys from the limo called me red and since I'm not a redhead, I assume it came from my choice of lingerie."

The carnie worker stepped up to our car and released the bar holding us in. Rett hopped out and took my hand to help me. His kindness and good manners never escaped my notice, but nothing he did said anything other than friendship. If he only realized how happy it made me to not feel like I had to act like our time was anything more than it was—two friends having a good time together. He understood this fact from the beginning.

Becks

Chapter 3

Walking back to the hotel where Rett stayed while we slept on the bus out back, we talked about nothing and everything. Our time together always had an easy vibe to it.

"Yeah, we need to get started on some new music. The label screams more music after we've been on the road. I guess those suits think we sit around doing nothing but holding a guitar or sitting at a piano when we're not on stage."

I laughed. "Isn't that good news though? I mean, it could be worse. They might say this was your last tour because they planned to cut the band loose when the tour ended."

He abruptly stopped midstride. "The hell you say, little girl. Bite your tongue. Those words need not exist in your vocabulary right now."

I stared at him. "Dude, I'm just joking with you."

His look scared me, then he started laughing to the point he bent over putting his hands on his knees. "I knew you were but it was too easy to set you up. You need to learn to not be so gullible, Skyla."

I wanted to laugh with him but I knew what he said to be the truth. "I know. I know. Sometimes, it can be a pain."

"Speaking of that... you want to come clean about what went on to get that lovely shade of red glowing on your cheek when I found you?"

"No, not really."

He stopped walking and took my hand. "I told you before I'm a good listener. You know you can tell me anything."

"Yeah, but this is personal."

"Good thing because I specialize in personal."

His gorgeous green eyes scanned my face as we stood still. I'd never talked to anyone about the situation going on with this tour. If I told him, the whole scene might crash down and I'd be the loser. I was always the loser with her.

"If I share this story with you it might end poorly for me. I don't know if I'm ready for my days on the road with the band to end."

"Who says they have to end? Sometimes I can accomplish a great deal without letting others know it's even going on."

"Oh, really? Like what?"

"If I told you that then others would know so... no can do." He tapped me on the nose and we started walking again. "But that doesn't mean something didn't happen."

"Like I said, this problem is personal."

"Did you slap yourself? Is it that personal?" His face scrunched up and he did that frown eyebrow thing again.

Becks

"We have a psychologist that works with the band from time to time. You know, if it's self-inflicted pain you're into. Does that have a name? Like cutting, only it's hitting instead?"

I shook my head. "No, I don't think so, but then since that's not the case it doesn't matter."

"Psychology interests me. I like listening to others and trying to help them."

"Thanks, but really, that's not it at all."

We reached the doorway to the hotel and the automatic doors parted allowing us to walk through. He headed toward the elevators and I stopped. The back door led out to the parking lot where my bus sat.

"Guess I'll see you tomorrow." I backed down the long hallway saying goodbye.

Before I turned he looked over at me, and it dawned on him I wouldn't be going to his room. He must be used to women spending the night in his room but that's not what would happen with us.

The friend zone had a lot of advantages, and it made me happy that's where I stood with him. As nice and understanding as he could be, I knew he didn't see me any other way. The ease of our evening helped get me past the hard time I'd had before he found me crying.

"Come up to my room and hang out. It's too early to go to bed."

"I bet you say that to all the girls." I smiled.

We joked earlier about him and the groupies so we both laughed when he looked at me.

"No, not really. Only the ones I want to have serious conversations with at midnight."

"Serious? I don't like the sound of that, but I do hear my pillow on the bus calling my name."

"I have goose-down pillows in my room. You can rest on one while we talk." The pleading sound in his voice caused me to cave. *What was it about this guy that made me want to spend more time with him?*

The ride up to his floor went quickly. He had his key ready when we stepped to the door. Before we walked in, the elevator opened and a wild group tumbled out, obviously intoxicated.

"Dude, hitting the help?" the drummer, Keller, yelled out. The guy's hearing must be failing to talk so loud. Hitting drums most of his life must be doing all the damage.

Rett let his door shut as we stood in the hall. "No, man. We went to the carnival I spotted when we came into town. Had to park my bike back at the venue so it could be loaded. We're just getting back."

"You should have come to the after-party." Keller's eyes cut to the voluptuous women standing under each arm. "Plenty of hot chicks to go around tonight."

Rett smirked at his comment. "Looks like it."

"You could've brought back a couple, too."

Did the dickhead think so little of me?

Was I not good enough to spend time with his bandmate?

"Shut the fuck up, Keller, you're being rude to Skyla." Having Rett come to my defense made me feel somewhat better, but still, the drummer had no reason to talk like I wasn't standing right there.

"Not rude. Just saying. The chicks at the party were all looking to add a dick pic to their rockstar conquests, and I know how you like to love 'em and leave 'em."

"I wanted something different tonight, dude."

Keller didn't reply but looked hard at me before doing a little nod of his head. "K, dude. Have fun." He stumbled off with the two barely clothed women to his room. Their laughter reaching the same pitch as it was before.

Rett waved the key at the lock. "Don't mind him, he's drunk."

"I can go so you can join them. That fake redhead eye-fucked you the whole time. I'm sure she'll be glad to add you to her list he talked about."

"Pass."

"Pass? But the gossip is you have a woman in every city."

"I don't give a shit what gossips say or think. I mean, I know there are people on this tour who spend their time leaking information to the press. It's what they get off doing or they make a few bucks extra. Who knows?"

"But you're not denying the rumor. Do you like living up to the stereotype of the bad boy rocker?"

He shut the door behind me and set the lock before he thought about finally replying to my comment. "I'm not going to deny it, if that's what you were thinking, Skyla. I've taken advantage of the situation from the first night on tour. I don't see myself as a bad boy rocker, though." He walked over to the minibar and took out a cold beer. Holding it in my direction, he offered it to me. I shook my head. The last thing I needed right now was to start drinking.

His comment made me wonder how many women he'd been with since we left two months ago. *Did he take the night off to spend a boring evening with me?*

His long body relaxed as he sprawled out on the soft white leather couch. The long draw on the brown bottle satisfied his thirst. "I'd have to be a lot worse to be called a bad boy rocker."

"Oh yeah, like what?"

"I've never trashed a hotel room or smashed my guitar on the stage. My guitar is my baby. I'd never hurt her."

His comment made me laugh because I knew his words were never truer. He loved the tone of the wooden instrument. Hence the reason he came to loading in and out most of the time. Making sure that guitar found its way safely into the stand from its case was part of his routine. Dex usually handled it himself for other bands.

"Good to know, Rett."

"Yeah, I've got my share of tats and sometimes I demand certain things be done a particular way but that doesn't make me bad. It makes me happy. I like knowing my equipment is taken care of."

"So wrecking things and getting tats makes for a bad rep, huh?"

Becks

"Hell yeah. The wrecking does, it also costs money, and the PR team goes all ape shit over getting ahead of negative press to do damage control."

Talking about our everyday lives came natural to both of us. We'd been this way since we first met. The casualness and relaxed atmosphere helped me feel like we lived normal lives. Being on the road every day had a way of making me crazy. I'd quickly found the cubby hole they called my bunk, started making me claustrophobic after a few weeks.

Rett reached for a remote and turned on some soft music. "You've managed to skirt around the conversation we need to discuss, Skyla. Who left a mark on you? Someone on the tour did that and they need to go. It would be irresponsible of me to sit back and do nothing."

My palm automatically cradled the hurt cheek. What he said was true but talking about it wouldn't miraculously make it better. The person who assaulted me refused to change. She and I both knew that. The abuse had gone on for so long now.

"I know you feel that way, Rett, but talking about it isn't going to stop the problem."

"Like hell, it won't. I'll have that person off the payroll in a heartbeat." The look on his face told me he meant what he said.

The silence in the room became overwhelming. Taking a deep breath, I let it out slowly.

I needed to trust someone with the information, but was Rett the one?

"Look, Skyla. I get it. You think you need to protect this person for some strange reason... a friend, a colleague, a relative... I don't know who or why, but can we at least talk about it? Make me understand why you feel that way. I'm a pretty easy going guy and a good listener. Tell me what's going on."

When I didn't answer, he continued, "Believe it or not, my life hasn't always been easy. I grew up in some fucked up conditions until my parents adopted me. The biological people who filled out my birth certificate, you know the sperm donor and the incubator... yeah, didn't want me. I lived in hell until I turned five and child services took me away. Sending me to school caused the 'rents all kind of problems.

"That month of September changed my entire life. They took me away, locked them up in jail for a while and sent me to new parents who loved me unconditionally. My mom and dad taught me the meaning of love. They instilled values I hold near and dear today. So when I say, I understand, I absolutely do."

The story he told shocked me. Rett never let on he'd come through something traumatic as a child. If others knew it they didn't share the information. I realized I was staring at him trying to decide what I could tell him.

I decided to start with the obvious. "I'm sorry that happened to you, Rett. No child deserves what you must have gone through. We don't ask to be born and choosing our parents isn't an option."

Becks

"What happened to me... yeah, I put that to bed a long time ago. We all went to counseling to deal with it and we did. They never tried to shove it under the carpet and pretend it didn't happen. We talked about it, cried about it, and then got over it. Life is what you make it and people have choices. I chose to let it go and be happy."

This statement made me smile. I wanted to choose happiness, too.

"Skyla, you can be happy, too. Let's deal with this toxic person and get them out of your life. I'm offering my help. Hell, I'll call my parents and they'll help, too. It's the kind of people they are."

"But getting this person out of my life is going to cause a huge ripple effect on others. It can cost me everything." I stood and walked around. "You don't get it, Rett. This person can create havoc on so many people I love if I speak up."

Before I realized he was standing behind me, he spun me toward him. The quick movement startled me but he held me still by my arms.

"Skyla. Listen to me. This person needs help if they think abusing others is okay. Let's do something to start their change. But for your sanity and mine, we need to get them away from you. Who knows, if they're hitting you then they're probably abusing others, too."

I shook my head. "No, I doubt it. I think she saves it just for me."

"Who. Is. It? I'm not going to let this slide so you might as well spill." Looking down at me his stern eyes took on a softer appearance. "I feel like I'm having to be a bully to get this out of you and I never want you to see me that way."

He let go of me but didn't move away. My body hated losing the warmth of his hands where they touched me. Bringing my face up to his, I watched him transform the look into something tenderer, more caring.

I sucked in a deep breath and let it out. "Okay. Can we sit down, though?"

Taking my hand, he led me back to the cushy leather and we sunk down beside each other. His hand never left mine. Instead, he squeezed. I glanced down at the connection. It gave me strength. This bond was something I needed to continue if I decided to tell him everything.

There was no urgency, his patience evident in the way he stayed silent simply holding my hand. His warmth against my palm calmed me.

When my breathing evened out I peeked over at him from the corner of my eye. *How did I get so lucky?* I mean, here I sat with this gorgeous superstar in his hotel room. He had no expectations for the evening other than to have some fun.

Our time together felt natural, unscripted. Two regular people doing normal things like going to a carnival, riding rides, winning crazy little monkeys to give away to the children. We laughed. We shared blue cotton candy until our lips looked like Oompa Loompas. I believed it was one of the happiest nights of my life.

Becks

Did I want to ruin it with all the negativity I was about to spew?

"Are you sure you want to ruin this evening with my bad shit?"

"The only way it's going to be bad shit is if it continues. Let's get it out and deal with it. Tonight. If we get this moving in a positive direction we can be done with it. Your life might be better for it." He squeezed my hand again.

I huffed. "Okay." Then nothing. *I thought of all the things I could tell him but did I want to?*

After a few seconds or maybe minutes, I felt him staring at me. "Whenever you're ready. I'm here."

"All right, all right… I'm trying to decide where to start."

"Why don't you start with who did it?"

I turned moving my knee up on the couch and sliding my foot under my bottom. Looking at him might be easier. He held my hand, though. The warmth making it easier.

"I'll start there, but you have to promise me you'll hear me out before you do anything. The whole story and the ramifications of what will happen to a lot of people must be heard before decisions are made. Do you promise?"

He twisted his lips as he considered what I said. Finally, he nodded. "Okay. I'll hear it all first, but make no mistake, Skyla, something *will* be done. I can't have someone working for me being abused by another person. It's not right. You know that."

"I know. I guess deep down I've always known. It should have ever gotten to this point."

"So, that might be the next thing to talk about. Why did you?"

"Right." I released a slow puff of air. "The person who did this is a relative."

"We have one of your relatives working for us?" He did the eyebrow scrunching thing. I wanted to smile since I'd come to recognize the look.

"Yes and no. She's part of the opening band." I stopped with that detail. I felt like I needed to weigh each word I said and decide what repercussions this knowledge might have.

"Are you going to make me drag every damn detail out of you, Skyla?"

"No, I'm getting there. Don't rush me."

"Right, yeah, there's no rush." I knew he wanted me to be forthcoming with this but spilling it all would take a lot out of me. "Whenever you're ready, I'm listening."

"The truth is… my sister is a backup singer for the first opening act, Flawed. She's traveled with them for a while now hoping to start or join a bigger band someday."

"Your sister? How did I not know this already?" He let me go and went for another beer. Looking over the bar top of the kitchen, he acted like he wanted to say more but thought better of it.

"We look nothing alike, but yeah, we are sisters."

"Which one is she then? Don't they have two?"

"Yeah, she's the taller one with black hair." My hair never looked the same from week to week. I liked colors so I changed it often. This week it was gray fading to purple.

"I know the one." His face contorted to a strange look.

"Please tell me you haven't slept with her."

"No, no, no. Nothing like that, but I'm pretty sure she's slept with some of the other guys in my band."

"I'm sure she has. She told me she likes variety. Personally, I think she believes it'll help her career to know and be with different guys."

"I don't think sleeping around is the best way to connect with people if you're planning to move up in this world. Lots of people go that route, though. Me, I can't do that."

"Yeah, me either. Not that I aspire to move up in the roadie industry." We both laughed.

He sat beside me, taking my hand back in his. Touching him seemed perfectly natural tonight, something we'd never really done before.

"Okay, so we know that you don't plan on being a roadie forever. That's a good thing."

"Correct. It's not something I aspire to be in for too long."

He looked at me. "You're not changing the subject, Skyla. We're so not discussing your career choices. At least not tonight."

"Damn." He squeezed my fingers together. "My sister is a lot older than me. My parents never said it, but I always thought I was an accident. Angelica sure enjoyed telling me it often enough growing up and my parents would scold her for her hateful words. They didn't deny it, though."

"That's rough. I'm sorry."

"I'm over it. You grow used to hurtful words after a while."

"I guess you do but it doesn't make it right."

"Anyway, she's ten years older than me and they always treated her like a princess. She regarded me like Cinderella and she was the mean stepsister, except she wasn't."

"Good thing there's only one of her then."

I giggled a little. Sometimes her behavior was mean enough for two people.

"My parents saw the situation as a built-in babysitter on her part, though. They left us alone all the time. Some of my earliest memories was of her being the boss because they went out with friends. She ordered me to wait on her, and I was too small to reach anything. It didn't take me long to figure out how to pull a chair over to get what she wanted."

"That's just wrong. Didn't your parents see any of this?"

"Oh, no way, she played them at every turn. If I said anything to them she quickly made up an excuse to cover it up. The next time they left though, she made my life hell. I can't tell you how many times the bitch locked me in a dark closet."

"That's so wrong, Skyla."

"You're telling me. Do you know how terrifying it is when you're five and locked inside a dark room while she tormented me from the other side with spider stories?"

"Her behavior's demented for someone only fifteen years old."

I agreed with him by nodding my head. "Right. Anyway, she'd lock me away for a little bit and then open the door. She'd tell me the next time I told I'd be in there for hours. Needless to say, I hardly ever said another word to our mom and dad."

"I'd have probably been having nightmares and they would want to know why." He let go of my hand and wrapped his big arm around my shoulders pulling me closer to him. The hard muscles holding me close should have relaxed me from the comfort he offered. Instead, the hold made me more nervous. I told myself to relax, he was only trying to help but damn, my female self was screaming '*holy hell, this feels good.*'

Taking a calming breath, I started again. I needed to keep my mind off his warmth, strength and fragrance. A trifecta of feelings assaulting me at once might prove too much.

"This continued until Angelica finally left for college. She stayed home for the first two years, so she was almost twenty before she got out of there. She majored in voice and got her degree, but she's never been able to find the job that will make her the star she aspires to be. My parents allowed her to move back home after college. That's when the problems for me started all over again. Thank God, I'd grown up enough to fight back though, but she got cleverer at hurting me. Most of her abuse was verbal by then."

"That's not any better, but at least you didn't have to defend yourself physically all the time. Your sister was a grown woman and you were still a kid."

"Yes, and the things she said to me was a lot more damaging to an adolescent. She basically destroyed my ego. To make matters worse, she instigated a lot of problems between my parents. They almost divorced over some of the lies she told them. It caused so much division between them."

"Didn't they see the shit she caused?"

"Finally. They still didn't want to believe she hurt me in any way, but they did see the problems she caused for them, so they made her move out. I danced around my room while she packed her stuff. Of course, my door stayed locked." I smiled and he laughed. My attempt to lighten the conversation a bit worked.

"I'm really sorry you've spent your life with someone so vile, Skyla. We can easily replace the band with another and get her off this tour. Flawed's music draws a good crowd but so do lots of other bands. They can be replaced in a flash."

"No." My voice went up a few octaves and louder than usual. "I'd never want to be responsible for them missing this opportunity of touring with Sharp Edges. The exposure they get from being with your band promotes them into famous territory, Rett."

"But not at the detriment of you, babe. Your life is worth far more than that."

"That's super nice of you to say that to me but we both know Angelica would never see it that way. I can't imagine the hell she would reign down on me if she figured out why the band lost the tour. I might not live long enough to find another career if she knew."

"Well, we'll look into it." He palmed my cheek. "Now, tell me, what caused her to leave her handprint on this perfect skin tonight?" The side of his finger slid up and down the area Angelica marred. While the ends were calloused from the guitar, the part he caressed on my face with felt smooth and soothing. I couldn't help but look at him while he touched me.

Reading more into the contact than I should caused me to break our eye contact. I felt the color rising in both cheeks as I turned my face downward. The light strokes warmed me in more ways than I wanted to admit to either of us.

"Skyla?" He lifted my chin with the same fingers. My heart said the look in his eyes was more than just concern but my head knew better.

"Yes?" The one word was all I could manage.

"I asked you a question."

Oh, right. He did.

"She claims I caused her problems by hanging around in the wings waiting to start pulling their set. Said she couldn't concentrate on her performance with me fidgeting where she could see me."

"That's bullshit and you know it. You were doing your job. It's another reason she needs to go, Skyla. You're paid to do a job, and she's stopping you from doing it if she's telling you where you can and can't go backstage."

I knew it. While I was making googly eyes at him, he was thinking about my crazy sister. What a dumbass I am. I popped up off the couch. "It's really late. I better go to the bus, I need to get some sleep." Before he could say anything, I took off through the door. I needed to put some space between the two of us before I made a bigger fool out of myself. The elevator doors opened as I stepped up to push the button making my escape even faster.

"Well, well, well… what do we have here?" Keller stepped from the elevator. "I knew Rett wouldn't pass up an easy piece."

My eyes instantly dropped to the floor as I moved into the empty space he vacated. That's what the band will all think now. I felt sure Keller would enjoy passing the news around about finding me here.

Maybe I was the one who needed to leave the tour?

Once again, Angelica would win.

She'd get what she wanted and I'd be left behind.

Making my way to the bus, I started making a plan of how to get off the tour and on another. I didn't need to lose my job, only this one. Lots of other bands had tours happening simultaneously. Hopefully, I could join another quickly.

I climbed onto my bunk and pulled the curtain shut. Grabbing my phone, I brought up the website for our company. Jobs were listed through the portal and I planned to check them tonight.

No use in wasting time.

Becks

I needed a new band and from the listings there were plenty requiring help.

Chapter 4

I woke up to the rocking of the bus moving down the highway. No noises could be heard inside the bus, so I knew everyone still slept. Climbing down, I made my way to the closet-sized bathroom. I wanted to bathe, pack, and be prepared to get off as soon as new positions hit my email. I prayed it would be this morning, and we would be in a city with an airport or a bus station where I could leave from.

Looking in the mirror over the miniature sink my first thought was the mark she'd left was gone from my face, but not from my head. I was a grown-ass woman. Why did I allow her to continue to harass me? The old hurt was still there. It was ingrained in me. The best thing to do was put distance between us.

If I made a conscious effort to check bands' tour schedules, I could be sure our paths didn't have to cross. I hated changing the teams I worked with, though. These guys knew me. They understood how I liked to do things. We'd spent some time building trust with each other. Having them depend on me to get my part of the job done took time to earn. Now, I'd be starting all over again.

That was okay, though. Knowing I never had to see Angelica again made me breathe a little easier. As I finished up my packing I thought back over the wonderful night I'd had with Rett. Our time spent together at the carnival played like a movie reel inside my head. We laughed and talked, and the evening seemed magical.

He probably didn't give it another thought after I rushed out of his hotel room. I was sure Keller had lots of nasty comments about me being in Rett's hotel room but I quickly shook away those thoughts because his words only added to my hurt. I didn't want to remember anything but the good from my evening with Rett.

From the noises I started hearing, I knew others were now awake and moving around inside the bus. I kept my curtain closed with my stuffed duffle bag sitting at the foot of my bunk. Talking to the others about why I was leaving was not something I was looking forward to. I hoped to avoid it altogether if possible. If the job came through that I had requested, then I'd be gone before they figured it out.

Lying back on my pillow, I tuned in music on my phone's playlist and put my earbuds in to listen. The constant lull of the bus swaying and the soft tunes of Jack Johnson I had programmed, let me drift off to some more much-needed sleep.

Thia Finn

This day could end up being a long one so sleeping was a welcomed thing.

***

"Knock-knock, Skyla." The sound of someone's voice jolted me from the delicious dream which had captured me.

"What? I'm asleep."

"Wakey wakey, little girl."

I knew that voice—*Dex.*

Guess he got the word I wanted off the bus, the very thing I wanted to avoid.

I slid the curtain back enough to stick out my head. "Morning."

"Glad to see you're awake. We need to talk." He stood staring at me waiting for a response.

Looking up at him, I decided to face the music. "I'm getting up. Give me a sec, please."

"Sure thing. Coffee'll be waiting." The bus lurched causing him to lean to the side as he made his way down the center aisle.

"Ugh!" I fell back on my pillow and wrapped my arm over my face. "Get up, Skyla. He's not going away." Only my own two ears heard the complaint. I rolled out of the bunk and hit the bathroom. Using my fingers I brushed them through my hair after going to the restroom and washing my hands and sleep from my eyes. The bloodshot look staring back at me in the mini-mirror caused me a slight flinch.

Becks

Once I was finished I quietly slipped up to the front where Dex sat watching a football game being repeated on ESPN.

Gradually my coffee cup filled as the Keurig did its job. Dex had the good sense to not talk to me when I walked in. The first cup happened before any conversation could be had.

Setting my hot cup on the table across from him, I wrapped both hands around the thick paper to absorb some of the warmth. The guys on the bus believed there was only one temperature for the thermostat to be set on and it hovered around sixty at all times, so I wore a jacket constantly.

"I got an interesting email this morning, Skyla."

"Oh yeah? From who?" I kept my eyes on my cup not wanting to acknowledge his statement.

He leaned in toward me. "Don't play dumb, little girl. You know exactly what I'm talking about."

I glanced up and met his eyes. No doubt he was angry but this was my choice. "I was going to tell you, but I thought I had some time before they notified you."

"My only question is why? Why do you want to leave this group? We all get along pretty great, I thought. Is there something I don't know about? Now's the time to tell me. This change isn't etched in stone, yet."

Here we go again. Why did I constantly have to justify my life to others? "No, there's nothing going on."

"After the text I got from Rett yesterday, I know you two went somewhere. I heard you were also in his hotel room."

"So. That's no one's business but mine. He told you I was going with him. I didn't ask for the time off. I actually told him no because I had to work but he insisted."

"Sounds like you didn't want to go with him then. Is that the problem? I've never heard anyone complain when a band member wanted to take them out for the night, especially not with him. Rett's a good guy."

"Did you hear me say he wasn't or the problem was with him? No. Rett's been a great friend to me and that's all. Yes, I did go to his hotel room. No, we did not sleep together. No, we don't plan to sleep together because we're good friends and that's all we'll ever be." I finally took a breath.

Getting all pissed off first thing out of bed made me go from zero to bitch in like two seconds.

"Does that answer all the questions you have now?" I glared at him across the table.

"You said the problem was not with him, so who's it with? We can straighten it out and you can stay with this team." Guess my glare wasn't badass enough since he didn't back down from asking more questions.

"I didn't say there was a problem."

"Yes, you did, Skyla. You said and I quote, 'or that the problem was with him.' That tells me the problem *is* with someone. Should I call Rett and ask? I'll take the risk of waking him because since you two were together, I bet he knows the situation."

Becks

"Dammit! Why can't people just stay out of my business? I need to quit this tour, Dex. Can we leave it at that?"

I waited for him to answer me. We seemed to be in some sort of staring contest forever. His hand scrubbed down his face like he didn't want to answer me.

"Part of me wishes you'd just let me handle this situation, Skyla. You're a great worker and losing you will be detrimental to the team we've established, but I get it. If there's someone doing something that makes you feel this uncomfortable, then I'll sign off on you leaving. Have you thought this through and not made a rash decision?"

"You know I have, Dex. I wouldn't choose to leave if there wasn't a real problem."

"Running doesn't always solve problems, though. Sometimes you need to buck up and face them head-on. What about this one? Is it so bad you can't do that?"

I took another deep breath and considered what he was saying. Facing down my sister would never be an easy thing for me because it had been going on for such a long time. As a kid, I had no recourse. My parents would always take her side even being the younger child. They spoiled her at every turn. Angelica managed to twist words around and use them against me all the time, especially when she returned after college. She must have found like-minded people to learn more or maybe just different tactics.

Glancing back at him, I wanted to tell him the story. Dex had kids of his own and might understand the situation more than most. But by telling him he would get her in more trouble and she would lose her job. Once again making it my fault.

"Look Dex, I truly appreciate all you've done for me. I know bringing a female onboard doesn't always work out with a bunch of guys but you welcomed me. You've treated me like the rest of the crew from the beginning. I'm grateful to you for that because it proved to the both of us that I could do the job." I stopped and looked out the window before turning and continuing, "I want to continue working in this field. I enjoy the work. I love traveling. Hanging out with a bunch of guys makes the days fun. Not having bitchy women to work with is even better. Right now though, there's a situation I'd prefer to not deal with, so transferring is the best thing for me. I realize I'm taking the easy way out but it's necessary."

He reached over and took my hand in his big warm one. "Okay, I'll sign off but know this, if you change your mind come on back, we'll be glad to have you."

His smile told me it was all true and I returned it. We both knew that returning probably wouldn't happen, but it made me feel better knowing he'd have me.

"Thanks, Dex." Saying more would cause tears so I stopped there. He squeezed my hand tightly and then let go standing up and moving to the couch area to watch the rest of the game.

I turned to the window and watched the scenery roll by.
Damn, I was going to miss these guys and the band.

Becks

My sister really had a way of screwing up my life over and over again.

Chapter 5

When my phone pinged, I knew it was the main office confirming my request. Glancing down I saw a text from an unknown number. As I read, I figured out quickly it was from Rett. We hadn't exchanged numbers so I wondered how he got mine.

Rett: *Saw in an email you're leaving the tour. WTF?*

How should I answer?

Instead, I threw my phone on the table. Did I have to justify my every move to other people? It pinged again.

Rett: *I'm not letting you leave Skyla, so answer me*
Me: *last time I looked you didn't have a say so. I'm going*

Rett: *No, you're wrong babe. I do have a say. It's our tour remember?*
Me: *I don't answer to you*
Rett: *I'll start over. Please don't do this*
Me: *It's the easiest thing to do, Rett. Don't make it harder on me*
Rett: *The busses are stopping shortly for gas. Come back to mine*
Me: *No.*
Rett: *Then I'll come to you*
Me: *No...*

Within fifteen minutes I felt the motor slowing down and we turned into a truck stop for fuel just like he said we would. I wondered if he'd arranged it. The man could talk anyone into doing anything.

The doors to the big rig opened and before I could stand up, Rett hopped up the steps.

"Did you make them stop?"

"No, our bus needed fuel and I'm sure if ours does then so do the others."

"But this wasn't a scheduled spot was it?" I watched his eyes move around the area instead of looking at me. Was he thinking up a good lie to tell?

"Well, maybe not but this works, too."

"So, you did convince them to stop. Why Rett?"

"I wanted to talk to you. It's been too long since I saw you." Full dimples appeared. This guy turned on the damn charm like no guy I'd ever known. It accounted for lots of panties dropping and some being thrown on stage. Why should I be surprised at how well he used it at will?

"Right, since it's been all of maybe twelve hours? Don't you have work to do or something with the band?" I heard him say something about continually working on new music when they were on the bus.

"That's why you need to come to my bus. We're hashing out some new music. You can listen in on how greatness is made."

I raised my eyebrows. "Hmmm... quite the modest rockstar aren't you."

His laughter caused me to join in. Laughing felt good after the morning I'd had. After chatting with Dex, my body wanted to go back to bed but I resisted. Sleeping away my troubles wouldn't work.

Rett reached out and took my hand pulling it to him. "I'd be honored to have you finish out the ride on my bus, Skyla. Please come with me." His eyes pleaded.

"That's not fair when you flash those green eyes at me that way. You cheat using them against me."

His lips lifted to that gorgeous smile again. "Did it work?"

God, this man. *How could I resist him when he pleaded with me?*

I took a deep breath and let it out slowly. I wanted him to know I was sacrificing my woman card giving into his charms this way.

"You know, you're not playing fair, right?"

Becks

"Skyla, you wound me deeply." He feigned hurt in his voice. "Do you think I am anything but sincere?"

"Sincere maybe. Playing all the cards to get your way, absolutely." I pretended to reach into my pocket and hand him something.

Rett looked down at my other hand. "What's this?"

"My woman card I'm handing over for your keeping. Giving in to you and all, guess you should hang on to it."

He took and pocketed it. "I'll take great care of it, for now."

Without dropping my hand, he turned and led me down the stairs of the bus. The sun shone in full force as we made our way to the band's bus. Riding all day inside I never knew how the outside felt. I liked the warmth shining down on me, made me feel like things were looking up.

I could only wish.

Maybe it was a sign that leaving was a good idea. I hoped so.

The door slid open immediately when he knocked on it. Guess his driver expected him back quickly. Rett certainly believed in his skills at convincing females to do what he wanted.

As I stepped up on the top rung, he started talking. "Guys, Skyla here is going to ride with us for a while. I wanted her to hear some of the new things we're working on."

The other two nodded, but Keller stood and looked me over from head to toe. Rett watched him as if he waited on the drummer's comment.

"Helllooo, Skyla." The way he drew out the welcoming sent the hairs on my neck straight up. I didn't know him well, but from the last time he spoke to me, my creep-o-meter started pegging out.

Rett quickly continued, "Keller, stop treating her like that. She's going to think you're a molester in the making." Turning to me, he added, "He's really the most harmless of us all. I guess first impressions aren't his best suit."

"Hey, I'm standing right here." He stuck his hand out to me for shaking. "Keller Westerly, drummer extraordinaire. Nice to meet you, Skyla. I might've been somewhat intoxicated the last time I saw you. Hope I wasn't too offensive."

Now he wants to be nice? I wondered if all drummers ran hot and cold like him.

"No, ah… not too offensive."

Laughter broke out around the common area where they all sat.

"That leads me to believe you've shown her your bad side. Drinking only makes him more obnoxious, so don't judge him when he's got a bottle in his hand," Rett explained.

"Or a bottle blonde either," one of the others with a guitar added. "Those usually go hand in hand, though. It's like he loses his brains when he's around women and booze."

"You're assuming he has brains," another chimed in. "He's a drummer, remember? They don't necessarily have too many of those to work with."

Becks

"This coming from the bass player. Ha-ha," Keller replied to his bandmate's cruel comments.

"Okay guys, that's good. She gets the idea. You're all a bunch of douche bags and she now knows the truth." Rett tried to end the banter.

Keller continued though, "Are you taking up residence on our bus for a few days, or what?" His face swung from mine to Rett's. No one missed his implication.

My eyes cut to him immediately. The look I gave him must have said it all, but before I could speak Rett intervened, "Keller, you asshole. She's only here to listen. I thought I made myself perfectly clear when I introduced her."

"So, not a bed hopper in our midst?" He had the nerve to wink at me like it was all a big joke to him.

Oh, hell no. I'd had more than enough of this guy, first in the hotel hallway and now here. "No, Keller. I'm not a 'bed hopper' as you put it. I'm not here to get in anyone's fucking bed or have anyone in my damn pants. I'm here because Rett thought I might enjoy listening to the band write some new music. I'm not the lowlife, the party girl, the next one night stand, or the newest notch on anyone's fucking headboard. Are you beginning to get the picture now?"

Dead silence.

They all stared at me like I'd grown a third tit or something. I wanted them to know they weren't going to walk all over me.

My problems with my sister held enough of this kind of shit. I refused to let anyone else talk to or about me.

Why couldn't I use this voice and words with my sister? All of my immediate problems would be solved if I did. My life could be my own path for the choosing.

Keller moved to stand directly in front of me blocking the rest of the band members with his huge stature. "Hey, I didn't mean anything by it. I'm not that guy, really. Ask any of these dickheads behind me. Honestly, I'm sorry." He looked sincere with the apology. His features softened and took on a boyish look.

I felt like I saw the real Keller, instead of the one who tried to be the tough guy but only came off looking like an asswipe. I dipped my head once to let him know I heard him but he wouldn't get off that easily. His actions had to show me he meant what he said.

Thankfully, Rett spoke up breaking our stare down. "Can we get back to what we were doing now that you two have kissed and made up?"

"Yeah, there'll be no kissing either." I smiled around Keller's big body and the others gave me large grins in return.

I'd dodged a bullet on what could have been a bad situation. I shouldn't have allowed any of it to bother me. Let's face it, I wouldn't be staying here long anyway.

They gathered their instruments and picked up where they'd left off before the busses came to a stop. I perched on the edge of a bench across from the others as they huddled around a small table playing and writing. Rett's hand wrote and erased over and over. Watching the way they created their next hit fascinated me.

I only finished two years of college, but most of the classes I took came from in the music department. Nothing I learned resembled any of the steps they used to compose line after line of the song. Their skills amazed me and I knew I wanted to learn more, either formally or informally. Maybe learning from real musicians held more possibilities than any class in I's previously enrolled in.

Shortly before the bus came to a stop, the guys laid down their instruments and called it a day. Their manager scheduled a radio interview for them today and then they would be off to the venue for a sound check.

My cue to leave the bus came with a text on my phone from Dex informing me my plans had changed. I would be required to do this next show and then I'd be flying to Miami to meet up with the next crew. Rotating my chair, I looked out at the back of the bus through the huge window.

"Dammit," I muttered under my breath.

The guys busied themselves with storing their equipment and not paying attention to me. At least I thought so.

"What's the matter, babe?" Rett came forward and leaned over my shoulder.

"I have to work this show tonight with y'all."

His lips turned downward. "Is it that bad to work with us?"

"Sorry. It's not your band. You should know that by now."

"Right. You can't let her get to you while you do your job."

"Tell her that. Her internal GPS keeps me as the constant designated location."

"Then turn off your beacon." He took my phone from my hands and shut it down. "Now she can't text or call to find you. Stay here on our bus if you want. She'll never look here."

"And how am I supposed to work?"

"I'll tell Dex you're sick and sleeping in the bed in the back."

No. That would be a bad idea. Telling anyone I was in a bed on the band's bus sent all kinds of wrong messages to people. Without saying a word to him, I shook my head and he immediately understood my thoughts.

"The first thing I'll do is inform him that nothing sexual happened on the bus. He can't ask you to work if you're sick. You might've come down with the flu on the road."

"In a few hours? He'll never believe it."

"You've been stressed for the last twenty-four hours, Skyla. Stress does shit like that. He'll get it. I'll make him understand."

"I appreciate all you've done to help me. Honestly, I do, Rett, but I can't shirk my responsibilities when I'm trying to get another position." With my mind made up, I snatched my phone from his hand and headed down the steps.

The equipment truck backed up to the loading dock as I made my way to the rear of the venue. Dex had diagrammed each one. Where the band was scheduled to perform, marked locations of the various parts, so he could supervise the unloading in a controlled fashion. Otherwise, every unload would be chaotic.

Before I reached the side door to join the other roadies, Angelica stood beside me. Instantly, I was on the defense.

"What do you want Angelica?" I kept my eyes on the opening door as one of the team chocked it.

"Why were you on the band bus?" She stalked me as I moved around the area.

"Is it your day to keep up with me? How did you know anyway?"

"I have my ways. Stop and look at me."

"Can't. I have work to do, remember? This is my part of the performance, and I'm paid to work not talk to you." Picking up the cables, I moved to the other side of the room. She followed closely behind me as I unrolled them.

"Did you talk about me to them?"

I whipped around and finally stared at her. "Why would I do that? I have nothing to say about you to them or anyone." I dropped the heavy black line. "You didn't answer my question. How did you know I was on the band bus?"

"Don't worry about it. I have my ways of finding out anything I need to know about Sharp Edges." The look on her face told me all I asked. "Which one of the band are you sleeping with?"

She made a sound like she didn't know what I meant. "Who is it, Angelica?" She didn't have time to answer because Rett magically appeared beside me. I hadn't seen him since I left the bus. I should've known he was around, though. We were unloading, after all.

"Hey Skyla. Feeling better?"

The strange look I gave him must've said I wasn't ready to play to his lie, but Angelica didn't see it.

"Are you sick?" She feigned concern for me. "You should've said something. I'd have come sat with you."

I wanted to punch her with her disingenuous worry. Any other time, if I acted sick, she ran afraid she might catch something. Her ability to show consideration for anything related to me never existed until a hot guy stood looking on.

"Yeah, I saw her looking green earlier and brought her over to ride on our bus. She ended up listening to us rehearsing some new tunes. I guess it took her mind off of being sick because she seems fine now." Rett's skills at producing lies out of the blue amazed me.

"I'm fine now. Thanks for asking." The less I said with either of them around, the better for me.

Angelica tried to put her arm around my shoulder but I leaned over and took a plug that needed a receptacle.

"I've gotta get busy, guys. See ya later." Walking away, I left Rett to deal with my sister bitch.

As I moved to the next location on the stage, I glanced over my shoulder. He walked away right after me, and I wondered if he said another word to her.

Maybe I would ask him later. But it didn't really matter, letting it all go was a better idea.

Becks

Chapter 6

The door to the green room jerked open as I loaded some food on my plate. Caterer's lunches waiting for the crew always helped us to finish quickly.

Dex came through looking around. When he spotted me, he headed in my direction. "You changed your mind yet?"

My eyes wandered around the room to see who was listening. The crew wolfed down the food and paid no attention to either of us, so I felt safe in talking. "No. Why would I?"

"Maybe you've calmed down and realized you're making a mistake." He offered me a slight smile with the comment.

"I doubt I'll change my mind. Besides, I've already told the office I'm going, remember?"

"That can be changed with one phone call, Skyla."

"Probably not going to happen."

The door flung open again and I groaned. I probably shouldn't have especially in front of Dex. Angelica and the rest of Flawed walked in. She acknowledged me standing there like she did all of the other roadies, with disinterest. As far as she was concerned, roadies ranked a step above rats but barely. We scurried around doing the grunt work while the important people enjoyed life.

The lead singer wandered over to speak to Dex and me. The guy laughed a lot and seemed to generally be a happy person. He enjoyed being around everyone as far as I could see, so why did he keep my sister on his payroll? She hated people.

Angelica wormed her way between the singer and me and started talking in the middle of our conversation. Typical for her. I looked up at Dex and smiled before walking away. Getting into it with her was a no-go in front of this crowd just as much as being talked down to. A barstool emptied, so I grabbed it to nibble from my plate.

"She's something else, Skyla," a whispered voice sounded in my ear. If I startled easily, this would have been a disaster with a plate of food in front of me. As I wasn't, I nodded in response without turning to see Rett. That luscious scent surrounded me and I knew immediately it was him. My girly parts sat up and took notice.

We both followed her movements hoping she would avoid me. After filling her plate with carrots and celery, Angelica made her way around the room talking and laughing with everyone other than the roadies, that was except for Dex.

Sharp Edges' members walked in shortly after she did and caught her eye. The hair flipping and pawing on their arms and backs of each one caused me to turn away in disgust. Being sick took on a whole new meaning just from watching her actions.

"Looks like she enjoys making the rounds with the guys, too," he whispered again.

It made me happy he carefully said the comments. The last thing I wanted was for anyone to overhear them and report back to her. She's obviously connected with someone on the band's or my bus.

"So I gather, since she knew I'd been on your bus. Wonder which ones she's been with?"

"Good question. She hasn't been on it when I've woken up."

"I hate dealing with this, Rett."

"I get it, babe. It makes life difficult to have to constantly watch your back. Let me get rid of her. Maybe their band can find another singer."

"*No!*" I said it too loudly and people stopped and looked at me with Rett standing behind me. Everyone knew who I was talking to now which meant Angelica also did. *Great.*

Rett moved away almost instantly. *Was he mad or did he not want to continue our quiet conversation?* I missed him immediately which threw my mind into a spin. Our friendship meant too much for me to start thinking things in that way. I could simply miss a friend, right?

Becks

I dumped the rest of my food. Eating no longer appealed to me. I needed to walk away from this. I viewed her making a fool of herself with all of these hot guys, and it made me want to punch something. Being violent wasn't really my style, but she brought it out of me every time I had to be around her now.

As I reached to open the door, she grabbed the knob and turned it for me. "Hey, where you going?"

"I've got work to do." The door swung open faster than I'd expected and banged into my cheek with force. I knew immediately it would leave a mark.

"Oh, I'm so sorry. I thought you were going to move out of the doorway before I opened it." Her voice dripped with kindness. "I would never want to hurt you. Your team is such an important part of the show. We need you all." She went on and on apologizing quickly for everyone to hear.

I felt the tears form and tried unsuccessfully to keep them from rolling down my cheeks. Dex and Rett both appeared on each side of me in seconds.

"Get some ice, Dex," Rett spoke first.

"On it." He moved to the ice chest under the table.

"It's not that bad." I heard Angelica tell them but neither said anything to her.

Dex handed a towel holding the ice to Rett and watched as he applied it to my swelling cheek.

"I'm sure she'll be fine. Right? What's your name again?" Angelica added as though she didn't know me any more than the others.

Rett, never taking his eyes off of me barked, "Get the fuck out of here. You're done with lunch." The anger in his voice scared me because I knew his words would come back to haunt me through her.

"It's fine. Really," I quickly said. "She needs to eat." My eyes pleaded with him to not do this.

He finally looked at her. "Eat then. Don't you have a rehearsal or something starting soon?"

"Right, I do. I'll go now."

"No, eat your lunch," he told her with less anger than before. I knew he understood what I tried to say without speaking. His eyes never left mine while he gently held the ice against the pain that was radiating through my cheek.

"I'm fine. You can let me hold it now."

He didn't let go.

Angelica went back to the food line and then sat with the other backup singer. Her band probably knew what a bitch she was already.

"You think we should take her to the medic?" Dex asked in a soft voice.

"No," I answered before Rett had a chance.

"I don't know. Let's have a look." He pulled the towel away as he spoke. The noise he made frightened me. No mirror meant I had to rely on them for seeing how damaged I looked.

Dex shook his head. "It's pretty bad, Skyla. Maybe you should go let the medical people evaluate it."

Becks

"I'll be fine. The ice is helping already. I'll take some ibuprofen and it'll be great. Work still needs to be done this afternoon." If I gave in to it each time she did something to me, Angelica would win. I refused to allow that to happen.

"Yeah, I'm not seeing you working today or probably tomorrow. Your eye's going to be swollen shut. You'll be a danger to yourself trying to work."

"No, really? Are you sure?" Panic started to set in. If I couldn't work, how could I leave this crew in a few days? Those people wouldn't want me joining them until I was one hundred percent fit for the job.

"You can't work with your face like this. We aren't slave drivers, little girl. You're injured on the job. You'll hang out and rest until you can see out of both eyes." Dex made the decision with Rett nodding his head in agreement.

"I need to see it."

"I'll take her back to the bus," Rett told Dex who reopened the offending door and stood out of the way for us to pass. Rett wrapped his arm around my waist to lead me.

I tried to look through my eye but the swelling made it impossible. Damn Angelica. She fucked with everything I tried to do. The walk back to Rett's bus gave me enough time to talk myself into a wave of anger that wouldn't go away anytime soon.

When he opened the door and guided me upward, I tried to discuss working again with him. "I'll be fine. Just let the ice do its job and then this evening after the show, I can go do my part."

"Don't even think about it. Going inside the venue with all the loud music can't be good for your head. Is it pounding already?" Rett knew the answer before he even asked it.

The mirror said it all and I sucked in a breath. "How could she do so much damage with just a door?"

"You know she did this on purpose." It was more like a statement than a question. Standing behind me, Rett's reflection in the mirror above my own showed a concerned face. Was it for my injury or about his allegation?

"Hard to say. She stays mad about stupid shit all the time. I think she makes up most of it. When it comes to me though, it's a hard call."

"No, I think she did it on purpose. She saw me talking to you while you ate, she knew you'd been on the bus with me."

"Yes, she probably thinks we've hooked up, and it's where she should be instead of me."

"I'm sorry for causing this problem for you, babe. If I'd have thought my actions affected her in any way when it came to you… well, let's just say, I would rethink allowing her on the tour."

With a shaky voice, I softly said, "It's okay, Rett. You had no way of knowing any of it." Our eyes locked in the mirror. His sincere comment touched me deeply. No one had ever taken my feelings into consideration over my sister's. She always received the attention, all the first thoughts. My parents made sure her comfort came before mine at every opportunity.

Becks

Him thinking of me first tapped something in my heart I hadn't felt often, if ever. This beautiful, talented, understanding man stood behind me concerned for my health and well-being. The tears I pushed down from the pain resurfaced, but not because of the hurt or even the horrid bruising that donned my face, but from the idea that someone like him might think I'm worthy of his care, his devotion to helping me.

Lines formed down my cheeks as the salty drops made their way to my chin and fell. He slipped his hand up from around me and caught them with his fingertips.

"Don't cry, Skyla. I know it looks bad and probably hurts even worse, but it's going to be okay. I promise. I won't let her hurt you again." He wrapped me in his arms, pulling me back into his warm body.

I closed my eyes enjoying the feel of him holding me from behind. When warm lips touched the skin of my neck, zings of unexpected lust shot through my body. He nipped and bit and soothed softly with the tip of his tongue. The intimate feeling escalated my desire with each nibble.

His bedroom eyes met mine in the mirror, the green hoods expressing the same as mine. "Are you okay with this, babe?"

Answering him right then and there was impossible, so I nodded once. Our relationship had always been a friendly one. Before this moment this guy had bestie written on every action. Now, I wanted him more than I'd wanted another man in my life. I needed him more than any man before.

He slowly turned me around and looked at me. My face looked worse than it ever had and yet, the way he stared at me said he didn't care. He wanted me for me, not for my looks, or my body, or my talents.

"You have to know, Skyla, this wasn't my plan but I can't deny how I feel about you. I think we both only wanted or maybe needed friendship, but it's so much more in my mind now."

Again, I nodded. His forehead barely touched mine, probably for fear of hurting me. I felt his warm breath fan across my cheeks when he spoke. I breathed him in. It was sweet like the soft drink he'd had earlier.

His lips slowly descended until they brushed mine with a featherweight kiss. The fire in his eyes met mine before he retook my lips. This time the kiss was nothing soft and sweet but filled with passion and feeling. As his tongue slipped against the seam of mine, I opened to allow him room to explore.

My hands grabbed his shirt front and I tugged him closer. If this was happening, I wanted it all. He pulled my arms around his neck before encircling my body and aligned our bodies in a tight hold.

This felt so good, so right.

Part of me wanted to say we couldn't, but I knew that was wrong. We could. Nothing stood in our way.

He angled his head and sought out every part of my mouth. No one had ever kissed me this way before. We both held on and savored the exploration.

The back of my knees hit the bed as he slowly led me in that direction. He carefully lowered me down so as not to let our heads bang together in any way. His body captured me under him and it felt right. It felt perfect. The need in me for this connection grew stronger with each movement.

He pushed his hands under my ass and ground his hardness against the part of me that screamed the loudest for attention. The last time a man had me in this position was so long ago I couldn't remember it. This time with Rett, I would never forget.

A warm hand found the bottom of my crew t-shirt and he slid it up my side. "You okay with taking this off?"

He was actually asking my permission?

"Yes, but only if you take yours off, too."

His dimples sunk in as he leaned back and grabbed the neck of his tee behind his head pulling it off in one smooth tug. I reached down to pull mine up and he stopped me. "Let me, please."

I smiled at him. "I wouldn't want it to hurt you." Both of his hands took my hem and slowly slid it up my body. If he expected to find frilly lingerie under my work clothes, he would be bitterly disappointed. My plain nude bra and panties served me well on tour, especially since getting naked with a rockstar wasn't on my agenda. Today he was simply Garrett Haspen, a man about to make me feel perfect.

Reaching my head, he stretched the shirt, so it cleared my face without touching it. The gentle care he used told me once again that I was special, as though my comfort was important to him.

With him straddled over my hips, he removed the shirt and threw it over his shoulder. My labored breathing proved my excitement that started with the kiss was still lingering. His finger began at my chin and ran down my neck and over my chest which noticeably rose and fell causing my breasts to rise up even more.

Stopping at the plain edge of my bra, he took a detour over the swell of one breast and then the other.

"You're perfect, babe." He flicked the front closure open with a practiced skill I didn't want to think about. The cups fell away with his help leaving me exposed to a complete view. "Just perfect," he said again as he cupped both sides kneading and lightly squeezing.

Before he leaned over for his first taste, he rolled each hardened peak between his thumb and finger slightly tugging. His touch sent another shot of need down my body straight to my clit. God, it felt like heaven waiting for him.

His tongue circled the stiff, rosy pebble coating it before he blew a cool breath across it, causing my back to arch off the bed. I needed him more than ever at that moment. My nipples had always been sensitive, but when he worked them both I thought I might come from that action alone.

"Damn, Skyla. You like that?"

Becks

"Yes, you're making me want you so much." I put my palms over his and held him there while he lowered himself back to lying on top of me. My legs automatically wrapped around his waist. Thank God for yoga pants.

Being skin to skin gave me my first feeling of what having a body like his against me was like. His well-defined pecs and abs slid across my softer stomach. The friction it caused made the heat inside me escalate to a fevered pitch.

His lips and teeth worked their way down my body until he reached the wide band of the stretchy pants. I let his hands go so he could continue the blessed assault he performed on my senses. When he stopped, I glanced down to find him looking at me.

What a view I had. His long hair was down and brushed across my skin, his face slightly reddened from his lusty ideas, and the smile said *I'm taking these off, too.* This must truly be a panty-dropping smile, and I couldn't wait until they did.

He stuck his index fingers in the tops on both sides of the band. As he slowly started dragging them down my legs, he grazed kisses across my skin below my navel.

"Are you trying to kill me?"

"I was thinking the same thing. You feel smoother and softer than anything I've ever put my lips on, babe. I'm so hard now I might explode from my dick moving over the bed."

"Don't do that yet, please." I sounded like I was begging, but then maybe I wanted to beg.

"No, not going to happen that way. I promise."

He sat up enough to remove my pants completely. Nakedness didn't usually bother me, but the way he stared down at me I wanted to cover myself. His beautiful words kept me from it. He liked my body just as it was, so that satisfied me too.

"Damn, Skyla. You're gorgeous. Why do you hide yourself under clothes like these every day?"

I raised a shoulder in response while he took off his jeans and underwear.

"Maybe I don't want the crew seeing me as a female first. It's a hard enough job to get into much less having to constantly worry about how the guys see me."

He gave me a strange look. "Guess I never thought about it like that but you're right. Guys might see you as easy prey. If they only knew what you hid from them. Now, they'll never know."

Before I could respond, he leaned down and dropped a kiss on my lower lips. He eased back more and spread my legs to get better access to the spot we both wanted him to find. His tongue worked its way inside the folds seeking the swollen nub waiting to be teased.

"Holy shit," I managed somehow to get out. My hand automatically found his hair, and my fingers found his scalp raking my fingernails across it while he devoured me with his teeth and tongue.

He sat back on his calves lifting me to his face driving his tongue inside me over and over before he laid me back down and slid a single finger inside me. When two entered me as he manipulated my clit with his magic tongue, I exploded. I knew my body prepared for more as I felt the liquid coat my opening.

Before I came down from the wonderful orgasm he dropped his jeans, rolled on a condom, and sunk into me sending me spiraling into a second orgasm. I had never done that before. I knew later I would pray for this kind of sex to happen again in my lifetime because once like this was definitely not enough.

Rett leaned over and kissed me hard as he stroked in and out at a feverish pace. When the kiss ended, he stopped moving. "Sorry. I got carried away. It just feels so fucking good, babe."

"Why'd you stop then?"

He gave a little laugh. "I know, right? No, really, I almost came, and I wasn't ready for this to be over so fast."

"No, me neither but you're right. Feels so perfect."

Pushing upward, I felt him sliding in but not as deep as before. He continued this way driving me crazy. I wrapped my hands around his ass trying to pull him closer but he resisted my efforts. He stopped again moved back to his calves lifting my right leg and pulling it up his body.

"I'm worried I'm going to hurt you. This will keep me from doing so." The intensity he took me at increased with each pump. He toyed with my clit in this position. "Babe, you gotta come now. I can't wait any longer."

With the way he played my body I couldn't have stopped myself if I wanted to. Good thing I didn't want to because my toes curled, the muscles in my legs stiffened and the orgasm rolled through my body like a freight train.

His must have been the same because he immediately fell down beside me as he pulled out. All that could be heard was our labored breathing. Once we both breathed easier, he pulled me to him from the side, being careful to not touch my face. His chin laid on the top of my head as he pulled the blanket over us from my other side.

After covering me, he moved out to take off the filled condom and then returned to get under the blanket and back into the same position.

I felt like I'd won the lottery. Fucking and cuddling in the same romp. *What more could I ask for?* Maybe getting banged in the face was worth it. If I ever got to leave this crew at least these memories would always be with me.

***

I woke disoriented in the bed. Sitting up, I realized I didn't have clothes on but the soreness I felt brought all the delicious memories back. No other sounds came from inside the bus, so I knew I was alone. I stepped into the tiny bathroom, and the moment the water warmed enough to stand it, I moved under the spray in the shower.

Noises came from the other end of the bus when I shut off the water. My alone time was over. The door popped open and I screamed at whoever decided to come in. "Someone's in here, you know."

"Yeah, and if there was enough room I'd join you." Rett's voice calmed me.

"Is everyone back on the bus?"

"No, just me for now but the whole band's headed this way. I jogged out to tell you to get dressed." He held a towel up to me. "You probably don't want to step into the hallway in a towel with this bunch around."

"Absolutely not. There's no telling what they would think about us hooking up while they had lunch."

Rett's head jerked upward. "Hooking up?"

I pulled up my yoga pants and looked at him. "Yeah, I mean, I understand what this was, Rett. You don't have to sugar-coat it for me. You have different women all the time."

He took my shirt from me and helped it over my head and face making sure to keep it clear of the swollen eye. "Is that what you think? I brought you back here to have a hookup, Skyla?"

Looking at him carefully, I thought I saw hurt or maybe it was disgust on his face. "I get it, Rett, really. It's okay. We both got what we wanted."

"So, you think we just used each other to get off with an afternoon fuck?"

My boots required me to sit down to pull them on so I moved to the edge of the bed. "I don't get it. Did you think I would need romance and all that? I know what you do, Rett. You have different women all the time. All of the band does."

"No, all of the band doesn't. I can count on one hand the number of women I've ever brought back to the bus with me at night. The others maybe, but not me, and not in a long time."

The sincerity in his statement surprised me.

"I'm sorry. I just figured you all did that. We see women coming and going from the bus and hotel rooms all the time."

"Yeah, you probably do but not with me."

It wasn't my business to keep up with what members of the band did after shows or at parties. "Really, Rett, I am sorry. We're always so busy loading out after a show, I never thought about who had women with them."

"Well, thanks for that, I guess." He looked down seeing I was completely dressed. "You can go back to your bus if you want to rest some more."

And there it is.

He dismissed me, just like that.

"Uh… okay. I'll go see if the guys need any more help."

"No, you go to your bus and rest. You're still hurt and don't need to be working for now."

I looked down and nodded, then he walked away. After what we had just shared, he dismissed me coldly without another thought. When I stood at the doorway, I turned and looked back at him. He stared at me but said nothing.

I opened the door and walked out.

Climbing back on my bus, I opened my laptop and pulled up the company's website. The message accepting me

Becks

waited in my inbox. The other tour group knew about me already, my transfer had been approved. I could pay my own way, so it was a no brainer.

A sound caused me to look up. I knew the door had opened. My heart wanted it to be the person I called my friend long before we'd slept together. Maybe we could go back to that status. I needed Rett's friendship but probably not right now. Some time apart sounded better for some reason.

The curtain on my bunk jerked open and there stood Angelica.

"What the fuck, Skyla? Everyone seems mad at me because you were dumb enough to get in the way of the door. You know that wasn't my fault. Sometimes I think you sit around and think of ways to cause me problems."

As I continued to read over my options, she stomped up and down the hallway ranting about how stupid I was. This happened to be a normal rave for her, so I refused to actually listen.

She slapped me on the back to gain my attention. "You. Little. Shit. You're going to get me fired."

"No, bitch, you're going to get yourself fired."

For the first time, I actually spoke up.

This caused her to stop pacing and look at me. "How dare you talk to me that way? Who do you think you are? Just because you fucked the lead singer doesn't mean you're any more than you were before taking it up the ass like you probably did. Or was it sucking his dick? No, you're probably too much of a retard to do that, right."

I was so over this.

Done.

Finished.

Stuffing my laptop in my backpack I grabbed my phone, my packed bag, and took off down the center aisle with her continually screaming behind me. The ride-share app on my phone said the car I had summoned to meet me out front of the venue was parked there already.

Angelica stalked behind me all the way to the front where she watched me climb in. "That's right, you dumbass, run away. Run very far. I hate you. Just like always, you ruin everything in my life. The day you were born I told them to give you away. The perfect family existed before you came along."

Pulling the door shut hard, I gave her the finger as we drove off to the airport.

Escaping from both of these people, who had no reason to treat me like scum, hurt me. I wanted to belong somewhere and with someone.

Angelica and Rett deserved each other.

If she played her cards right he could learn to love her instead, since she was so much better than me.

Chapter 7

The plane touched down waking me from a restless sleep. All of my luggage rode above me so I was able to grab it quickly and walk straight to the Uber line at the Miami International. The car and driver waited, so I climbed right in.

"American Airlines Arena," the female driver confirmed.

"Yeah, thanks." I had texted Dex before I boarded the plane to tell him of my change of plans. My phone blew up when I took it off airplane mode but looking at the messages needed to wait. Dealing with that shit ranked low on my to-do list at the moment.

"You coming in for a big show tonight?" the young woman asked.

I knew the company encouraged them to talk to their riders to ease any anxieties the customer might be having. "Yeah. I work with a crew for the band."

"Whoa! That sounds like an awesome job to have." Her enthusiasm made me smile.

"I like it most of the time."

"I bet working like that gets to be like any other job, right?"

"Pretty much. It's not a nine to five but you learn to enjoy some parts of it more than others."

She glanced at me in the review mirror. "Piece of equipment fall on you or something? That's a nasty looking black eye you got there."

My laugh sounded cynical even to me. "Actually, it was a door. There's a perfect line down my face from the edge."

"That sucks. I bet it hurt like a mother…" She caught herself before finishing the descriptive words. "Sorry. We get warned all the time about using bad language."

"No problem. That would describe it perfectly."

She pulled up outside the arena and stopped. I gathered my things as she opened the car door. In her hand was a piece of paper she handed to me.

"It's my, uh… phone number. You know in case you run into any more doors while you're here. No one has to put up with that."

I stared into her blue eyes. She thought she understood my situation, that I'd been a victim of something bad. I hated to tell her it was a door and maybe it was sibling abuse. *Was that even a thing?* If so, I'd been abused both verbally and physically all my life. Mostly, I labeled it as bullying but wasn't that abuse too?

Becks

"Thanks. I appreciate you trying to help." I shoved the number in my bag and walked to the box office to find out where I needed to go to join my crew.

My new boss waited as I rounded the side of the building having been called by the office people to inform him of my arrival. They couldn't be too careful since people tried to sneak into venues all the time, especially women when a band of hot guys were performing.

Aaron put his hand out to me as I walked up to him. "Glad to have an experienced crew member join us. We've had to let a few go since we left New York."

"Thanks, I'm happy to be able to help out." I knew he studied my banged up face. "Yeah, about that... sorry, I know I look like an MMA fighter. Ran into a door that someone opened at the same time. The door won." Laughing it off was easy now.

"Hope the door looked as bad as you do or the person who opened it."

"I wish. The door was solid wood. My face took the worst of it." I laughed a fake laugh this time, praying I wouldn't have to tell the story over and over.

"Okay, let's get your stuff stored and I'll introduce you around. You sure you're able to work with that eye still swollen shut?"

"Yes, completely. I promise I'm fine." This lie might come back to haunt me but a bottle of ibuprofen hid in my backpack.

The crew worked together as I watched them. They each had their assigned duties, and Aaron told me for now I could watch and lend a hand where needed. Learning names and jobs happened quickly as I picked up on how each person liked to do things.

Once the stage filled up with equipment, cables, instruments, and cords, the group left for dinner. This time, another female worked with them.

She spotted me and stopped, inviting me to join them. "I'm Sarah."

"Skyla."

"Cool name, Skyla." She said it as though she tried it out on her lips. "I mostly work with the sound guys but you know we help everyone out."

"Right. That's what I'm used to also. I usually work with the guitars, but I don't know these guys and what they like, so I'll do whatever I'm told for now."

"Good idea. The guitar guy's kinda an asshole."

"Sounds like what I'm used to." We looked at each other and laughed out loud. Guess we both knew what it was like to deal with these types of guys.

The workers piled around the food and loaded plates down before finding a spot to eat. Sarah and I took our plates out to the stairs behind the building and sat down. This crew worked the same as my crew with Dex, so I knew I should be able to move into the job easily.

"Where were you before here?" Sarah took a huge bite of the taco she held.

Becks

"I flew down from Philly."

"Who were you working with?" I knew she meant the band.

"Sharp Edges."

She turned her head with her mouth hanging open.

I expected her response.

"You left those guys to come here to tour with us?"

Nodding at her, I knew what Sarah meant. The band she worked with had been around since the seventies. They still drew big crowds but the older members liked things done the old school ways. Convincing them to upgrade sometimes caused everyone to butt heads.

"Damn girl, I don't know what happened to your face and eye, but I hope they took you in for a scan. You lost some sense in that hit."

"No, I made a choice before this happened, so I'm pretty sure my brains are all still intact." I pointed to my eye. "This right here convinced me I made the right decision."

"Uh-huh. Was it a guy in the band then?"

I shook my head. "Nothing like that. Sharp Edges are all great. Well, the drummer can be an asshat when he wants to be, but the others assured me he wasn't like that all the time."

"Good to know if I ever get a chance to travel with them. I'd kill to be on their tour. Those dudes are smoking hot and their music makes me want to dance or maybe do the horizontal mambo anyway."

We laughed loud and hard. I liked Sarah already. The decision to change might be just the thing to solve my problems. Remembering to check schedules before each tour had to be a priority from now on.

With nothing to do until sound check, we went back to the bus. The other guys who hadn't left exploring the city sat around playing video games on the big screen or doing something on their phones. The empty bunk above my new friend worked for me, so I climbed in to store my stuff away.

Glancing at my phone as my head rested back on my pillow, I turned it on knowing the messages stacked up. I hated to face the music but couldn't put it off any longer. It surprised me to see only a few, and especially one from my sister. She sent a voice mail that made me want to hurl.

> *"Oh, my goodness, Skyla. Why did you leave without saying goodbye? I came to check on you and Rett told me you left to work somewhere else. Whatever were you thinking? Of course, he had a few other groupies under his arms so I didn't want to ask too much. He invited me to join them in his hotel but I declined. Can't be mixing work and pleasure, you know. Anyhoo, I'll try again later. Take care."*

I wondered who listened to this message while it was being recorded. She never left one that wasn't her bitching about something she blamed me for or something she needed me to do. An innocent bystander heard her sugar sweet tone and words I was sure. Well, maybe until she gushed about Rett's invitation. God, she made me ill.

Dex left a text wanting to know if I made the trip okay and to say he would take me back on his crew anytime. I appreciated his kindness, but as long as my sister was around that wouldn't happen. The team that continued to work with Sharp Edges would be a no-go, too. The last thing that appealed to me was running into Rett with other women.

His friendship would be missed because he was always understanding and a great listener. Our hook-up turned out to be a huge mistake on my part. If I could only go back and do that time over again.

Rett's name stared at me from the screen. Reading them would hurt because what could he say that was good? Would he be sad or happy I left? I feared the answer, so I didn't open them. Maybe if I faced them later it wouldn't hold so much pain.

As I rolled over and started my playlist, one of Sharp Edges' slower songs started. I kidded myself into thinking I would trade our intimate time together. Hell, I'd do it again in a heartbeat. His tender side touched me more than ever before. And the sex, whoa, damn well off the charts hot.

Slinging my arm over my face, I listened to his voice on the song and relived those moments with him. His touch, the deep kisses, the way he made me come over and over.

"Shit." I sat up before that happened merely from the memory. *Was that even possible?*

"Is something wrong?" Sarah banged on the bottom of my bunk.

"No, hit my eye accidentally. Hurt like hell."

"Girl, are you always accident prone?" Her laughter floated upward. Maybe it was partly my fault, and I jumped to the conclusion that Angelica did it on purpose. Blaming her was the easy thing to do since I'd done it all my life.

My phone lit up and then started ringing. Actual calls rarely happened so it surprised me. The I.D. said Bitch. "Guess she's got more people to impress with her gushing in the phone," I whispered to myself and made the mistake of answering it. "Hello, Angelica."

"Where are you?" The clipped tone she used told me something bothered her.

"In another city where you aren't." Responding to her with a smart ass comment came natural to me sometimes.

"You've done it this time, you stupid shitface."

Well, well, the true Angelica sounded like her normal self. She must be alone.

"Oh yeah. Guess you'll have to deal with it on your own. I'm not around to take your anger out on."

"I need you to tell me where you are so I can come to you."

"Not a chance in hell."

Why would I want her around me? She cost me the best position I'd ever had.

Becks

"Where the fuck do you think I'm going to go since you got me fired?"

"What? I left so you could keep your damn job."

"Like hell you did. You left because Rett couldn't stand to see you around after your little indiscretion on his bus. Did you think other people wouldn't know about your fuck fest with him? I was happy he kicked your ass to the curb until he decided seeing me around could be trouble."

"He didn't even know I left, Angelica. Dex and I made the reassignment. Rett had nothing to do with it."

"None of your damn excuses matter, slut. I have nowhere to go and not enough extra funds to get home. So, you need to fix this by sending me enough to get to you or home."

"See that's where you're so wrong. I owe you nothing. You caused all of your own problems, so you fix them. Call Mom and Dad I'm sure they'll gladly get you back to them."

"I don't need them to rescue me when you can't be that far."

"I'm in another state far away from you. I flew out." The last thing I wanted her to know was where to find me. I felt certain Dex wouldn't tell her, so I was spared dealing with her abuse.

"I have to go Angelica. Good luck to you."

Her screaming lasted until I pushed the red circle on my screen.

"So long bitch," I added before throwing my phone to the side and returning to my soft pillow.

Chapter 18

The show went off without incident and I pitched in everywhere I could to get everything ready to roll to the next venue in Atlanta. Sharp Edges had played Atlanta but at a different venue. Maybe I could see more of the city this time. The downtown area had some cool places to visit and their rail line made it easy to get around.

Sarah and I finished up and headed back to the bus area. We laughed about something funny one of the guys had said as we rounded the front of our bus.

I stopped instantly.

"What are you doing here?"

"Well, when you didn't respond to any of my messages I decided you must really be hurting and needed me."

Sarah watched the two of us. "Uh… I think I hear Aaron calling. I better check in with him." I didn't hear her walk away.

Becks

Rett took a step closer to me. My heart leaped into my chest. I felt it running a race inside of me.

"Babe. Why didn't you say goodbye?"

"How could I? You dismissed *me* if you'll recall. Sent me back to my bus. Alone."

His eyebrows scrunched together. Damn him for the looks he gave me. I knew he tried to remember his words. His thumb and middle finger squeezed his temples. "Yeah. I did. You pissed me off. I shouldn't have done that. I'm sorry."

As I tried to come up with the right words to say, he stepped in front of me. "Skyla, you calling us having sex for the first time a hook-up really hurt. First off, you're my friend and I would never treat a friend that way. Secondly, my feelings for you are deeper than simply being my friend."

His palm cupped my injured cheek so softly I barely felt the warmth coming from it. The green of his eyes almost glowed under the street light above the bus. They held me memorized as he continued to speak, "When I had you finally beside me sleeping, I knew then that we had busted the friendship barrier all to hell. I thought we were both ready to move forward with a stronger relationship and then you debased us both referring to it as a hook-up." He took a deep breath before continuing, "Don't you see, babe... I want you more than any other girl I've ever wanted. The night you ran after we were in my room I knew it, but I thought you ran because you wanted more time. I don't know, I guess to be sure."

The longing in his eyes, the sincerity in his voice and words melted me.

Could we do this and work together?

Would it last?

All of these questions roared in my head.

"Rett…" I laid my hand on his allowing him to touch me harder than he dared. "Are you sure? This is a huge step for me."

"Yeah, I know. It is for us both, but I'm willing to do what it takes to make it work."

"Work? What are you doing here? When the band is supposed to be playing tonight?"

"Stop evading my questions, Skyla. Do you want to give this a try or not?"

Tears formed in my eyes. Happy tears this time. "Yes, I want to give it a try. With you, with my friend, with my confidant, I'm ready to work for more."

"No more hook-ups?" he teased as he said it.

"Never any hook-ups. And you?"

"No more, hopefully ever."

He leaned in and kissed me softly, then pulled back. "Damn, I'm glad you see it my way."

The look on his face made me wonder about his comment. "Is there something you need to tell me, Rett?"

"Yeah, there might be." His panty-dropping smile eased across his face as the dimples deepened. "Your sister left today."

I glared at him out of my good eye. "Left or fired?"

"Maybe both?" He formed the question.

"Both, huh? How?"

"That's for her boss to tell you. In the meantime, your boss expects your cute ass back on his crew's bus in the morning when we arrive." He glanced down at his watch. "We need to get going to make it to the next location when they do."

"How are we going to get there that fast?"

"Leave that to me. I'm not a rockstar for nothing, babe."

Thia Finn

Acknowledgments

Thank you to Verlene Landon for allowing me to join this wonderful group of authors on this adventure of Escaping the Friend Zone. It's been a wild learning experience I'm happy to have been a part of.

Becks

Playlist

Check these out on Spotify or iTunes –
alt-rock Lives!

I love Alternative Rock Music. You never know what kind of sounds you're going to be introduced to. I listen to AltNation on Sirius Radio most of the time, but your local alt-rock stations are just as good. Check them out sometime.

Type your playlist here in the following format:
You're Somebody Else by **Flora Cash**
Angel Eyes by **TaxiCab Racers**
broken by **lovelytheband**
home by **Morgxn & Walk the Moon**
Over my head by **Judah & the Lion**

Connect With Me Online

Goodreads Links
Check out the books below and add to your TBR list.

Assured Distraction Series
Assure Her (Assured Distraction Book One) – Keeton's Story

His Distraction Assurance Distraction Book Two) – Ryan's Story

His Assurance (Assured Distraction Book Three) – Gunner's Story

Distracted No More (Assured Distraction Book Four) – Carter's Story

Hayden's Timbre (Companion Book to Assured Distraction Series) Hayden's Story

Fat Boys Series
Half sac
Lateral Moves

Becks

Website
http://www.thiafinn.com

Email
author@thiafinn.com

Facebook
https://www.facebook.com/ThiaFinn/?fref=ts

Goodreads
https://www.goodreads.com/author/show/14206242.Thia_Finn

BookBub
https://www.bookbub.com/profile/thia-finn

About the Author

Growing up in a small town Texas, **Thia Finn** discovered life outside of it by attending The University of Texas, only to return home and marry her high-school sweetheart. They raised two successful and beautiful daughters while she taught middle school Language Arts and eventually became a middle school librarian. After thirty-four years, she retired to do her favorite things like travel, spend time off-roading with family and friends, hanging out at the Frio River, reading, and writing.

She currently lives in the same small town where she grew up with her husband and their new Chihuahua puppy, Josie. She can often be found stalking on social media, watching Outlanders, Game of Thrones, and the newest Netflix and HULU dramas.

Made in the USA
Columbia, SC
08 August 2019